The Street

The Street

103 Sonnets of a Time and other poems

David R.A. Pearce

Published by: Apex

Printing support by:
Booklogix Publishing Services, Inc.
Alphretta, Georgia

Cover Photograph: David Woodnott; edited: Philip S.Hodges
Author photograph: Chris Tyson
Layout and Design by Scott W. Biddulph

ISBN: 978-1-63183-001-3

For Liz, darling-wife;
for Catherine, Stephen, Philippa, and Nicola;
my grandchildren, and for all dear friends
who have sought to make honours
of my impossibilities

That Love is all there is,
Is all we know of Love;
It is enough, the freight should be
Proportioned to the groove.

Emily Dickinson

'The Street', Whitstable

The tide is on the make.
Rustling wavelets, rank on rank,
Obliquely rasp and rake
The sides of this long shingle bank.
Twice a day across The Street
With steady urgency they meet,
Unravelling a prow of foam ahead
In criss-cross patterns where they spread.
Sheppey's bluff across the bay
Is sharper in the evening ray,
While eastwards to Reculver towers
The stacked onset of darkness lours,
And lights around the estuary
Half ring my patch of open sea.
Nor light, nor dark, nor sea, nor land:
Between uncertain worlds I stand.
One day, not now, I may not hide
From Time's encroaching, Night and Tide.

23rd March, 1994

'The Street', off Whitstable, is an enticing narrow promontory of shingle, shell and pudding-stone extending some mile, or mile and a half, into the sea. It is completely covered at high tide, with rising waters encroaching from both sides. One has to be careful not to be cut off.

Table of Contents
~Sonnets~

~Poems~

Preface

Just as disreputable lounge-lizards masquerade behind false identities, so these sonnets may not be what they claim to be. Are they sonnet imposters? Sonnets, we are predisposed to think, are about Love, with an inclination to high Romance. These poems, though, are written mainly within an eighteen-month period of a cancer diagnosis. Sonnet-love may often be with hope of fulfilment, but the subjects that exercise my mind are, in one sense, ridiculously futile and finite.

At first the medical outlook was entirely bleak, and if that had remained the case my reader would have been spared this autumn canter in the late sun. Never, though, have I been more aware of Love, and Beauty, and of Life's benison; and so these sonnets are a realistic celebration of family and friends, especially of my dear Liz who is my companion in all the ups and downs. I say 'realistic' because these poems do not balk at the inevitable. As many around me drop away, I feel my mortality. I realise that I live in stolen time. This makes this sonnet theme more intensely, and immediately, relevant - for me, at least.

A sonnet sequence needs a theme, and that theme has been set by my cast of thought and by daily routines and interests - the hidden recesses that I can disclose most easily on paper. All this may have little significance for you, as reader, but it is important to me. If these poems were not scrupulously honest, they would have no meaning, but as it is, they have helped to give me a purpose and, perhaps, a different kind of continuity.

That being so, I have little concern as to how they rate in any scale of judgement, though I do hope that they find some favour with friends, and, perhaps, give encouragement to those facing the same journey.

The sonnet framework is a great help because it concentrates the mind. I enjoy the restriction. It will be argued, however, that too much in these pages is condensed – cram-packed into fourteen lines- and fractured; and that meaning is not always clear.

The individual poems should be looked at as part of a whole, and that whole should be seen as a sunny landscape with occasional overshadowing clouds. That may help to explain what is individual and idiosyncratic in individual poems.

The inevitable criticism will be that the poems lack the musicality of genuine sonnets. Awkward punctuation and the turns of speech impinging on a proper wave beat of iambic stress will jar some sensibilities. The rhythms are not insistent but I hope they will be found. The patterns of rhyme are the chiming that I particularly enjoy – there is nothing like a sudden resonance of sound – and they, too, give me a discipline of structure.

Metre, rhyme scheme, and development of octave and sestet – of course, one should be aware of them all; they provide the ideal towards which to strive. The final Shakespearean couplet I have kept because I enjoy the snapped-shut conclusion, or the whimsical twist.

The poems are dated from the day (or night) when they were first conceived. The date is not that of their final form; and so, although there is a chronology, it is not often precise.

I daresay the purists will find fault and say that these are but sort-of sonnets. That is perfectly just because they represent a sort-of adventure.

David R.A.Pearce
17th April, 2015

The Boundary Line

Let me consider life to be a span
Decided, fixed, before I came to be –
Pre-dating babe, before the longed-for man –
And written in some book of Destiny.
I do not have to cogitate or dwell
On who or what devised my living's length.
Heredity or God? I cannot tell.
Or whence the years, or why my failing strength.
What matters is – **the boundary is set;**
And to that line my game is played to score.
Once crossed, then all is done; there is no more
To ask, for neither world nor I owe debt.
  So never shed regretful tear of grief,
    For Time has just its due, and is no thief.

24th May, 2002

6, Charles Street, and 'Flikkers'

for Mary Milne and John Davison

Houses, like dogs, unowned look sad, forlorn.
I pause by yours and see the curtains drawn;
The letter-box stuffed open with old post
Never to be read with breakfast tea and toast,
Amid brocade, fine books, and old-time airs.
A plant droops on a windowsill upstairs.
Paint peels. Here, yellow petals pink-blushed fall
From rose bushes that oversprawl the wall
Untidily. I cannot claim I knew you;
Edward Thomas did – but not at this address.
Now, 'Not at home' your silvery-graciousness,
Though sudden-bounding ambuscades renew
  Greetings from far, in portraits that prove
    Not in houses we live, but in other's love.

Summer, 2000

1

Death of a Dog

for Rupert, James, Larry, Ben, and Hamish

God – contemplating Man's impaired estate,
Its mutability and passage brief –
Gave him the Dog to inculcate belief
That he might grow accustomed to hard Fate.
Within his own life's span he might debate
Some six or seven times small bouts of grief,
And manlier face at length that subtle thief
Who for those, his dearest, always lies in wait.
Alas, divine intention fell well wide,
For that companion in adversity,
Though dumb, won such regard for loyalty
And trust, that every death was joy denied.
    In this we see God's primal logic slip,
    But none would change for cost that comradeship.

19th August, 1993, and 2014

Death of Donald V. Miller

You know when the tunnel is coming;
Nose-to-window-pane expectancy. Steam train
Travel. The signs. Wheels differently drumming;
Blurred lines of houses on a rising plane
Against the sky. In the country, shouldering
Embankments of ox-eye daisies blank sight,
Flatten the smoke, echo the thundering
As you hurtle towards underground night.
Old time-wise travellers anticipate
The sudden shock of air, blockage of ear;
Lean forward, heave the heavy window tight
Up, by the strap…and resume their paper.
    Breath-taking 'Whoosh'; the crossword put on stay:
    Hold tight. A short night's journey into day.

20th April, 2002

Mistress Mariner

Dear Mistress Mariner, I thought to trim
My bark with **Love** as ballast, set the sail
That it might hold my helmsman course, and skim
Regardless of the world's cross-tide or gale.
But when aboard we stowed your extra freight
Of **Love**, we drove too deep in heavy seas,
Nor could we gain some blank uncharted strait,
Nor 'Go about' for all your expertise.
Capsize we must, or make despairing shift
To jettison rich cargo o'er the sides.
In haste I cast my heavy **Years** adrift.
That done, the vessel rights itself and rides,
    And braced within, without, in sunset breeze,
    We hold due course for the Hesperides.

June, 2002

A Part to Die For

If I knew Time for me this day should cease,
Would I wring every instant to its core?
But how? Call round my friends, allot my store,
Forgive, repent, and face the dark in peace?
Or like the doomed slave in a Roman play
Condemned to die on stage in Art's blest cause
(A part to die for, but you miss th'applause!)
Mess up my entry, fluff my lines to say?
No, I shall hug you, wordless, to my side,
Twine fingers in your hair, and kiss your eyes.
Thus Time, or fast or slow, holds no surprise
Because its passage has been nullified.
    And this is true, for I have been before
    Clasped in that Love, contented at Time's Door.

10th July, 2002

'Time hath, my lord, a wallet at its back ...'

There must have been a world of other days
But they have foundered, are for ever lost –
Swallowed in the witching swirl of haze
Where the fierce Cyaneaean currents crossed
To bring Odysseus on the wrecking rocks.
Far other lotus hours by casual use
Just yield and fade, succumbing to the shocks
That leave no trace or heritage of clues.
Oblivion must claim the alms we treasure.
This day, though, **know** full worth of what we give;
Nor forwards, backwards, think to measure,
But simply live our love and love to live.
    One day we'll sit – our satchels 'tween our knees:
    And delving thence, know what it was to please.

January, 2003

For Sale. Job Lot

Old portrait postcards are the saddest things
Orphans belonging nowhere, lost, unloved;
No name. In bundles tied, in boxes shoved
Haphazardly, car-boot job-lot changelings.
Men in uniform, or promise-poised, stand
Beside a column or an antique urn;
Women, studied in what-they-think fashion,
Pose head erect; with gesture of the hand.
Thus they define a state, or contemplate
A play of life that plots no stratagem.
They look ahead as I look back to them;
And each of us already out of date.
    Their stories all untold, but what is worse:
    None now accompanies their funeral hearse.

February, 2003

Heresy

Though diary and these poems hang me yet,
The making this-world's-beauty my whole creed,
And building shrines of Joy to my soul's need
Are heresies I never shall regret.
Weak men write false confessions in the hope
That by conforming to conformity –
Denouncing what they are – they may go free,
And nothing counts but to escape the rope.
I write, and would again, and stand by still;
Nor choose to wear a more becoming mask.
If such you wish, some other actor ask.
You, reader, must construe for good or ill,
    And, from my silence make, mark, what you can.
    These words must stand for DRAP, who is but man.

28th March, 2003

Love's Blazon

for Mary Balfour

This is the reason that our loves exist:
T hat for the bleakest moments we prepare,
And by dear preludes of delight and prayer
Ensure, now, sadnesses-to-come be kissed
Away. The savour of my life is missed
If I hope weather should be only fair;
Naively think that never needless care
Will lie in wait round my enraptured tryst.
Roll all you loved into one golden ball –
What once was perfect must be always so;
You are not less for having once owned all –
Then toss it high that all the world may know.
    Love's blazon shines in faces that have dared.
    You trusted so; and, daring, sharing fared.

30th March, 2003

'And Nothing brings me all things'
Timon of Athens.

The day my mother died

If all my life showed riches as my grief,
Then none should beg for alms from me in vain;
I should make honest every wayside thief;
Leave usurers to mutter and complain.
But **now**, my capital investment lost –
My argosy lies wrecked upon the shore –
I have no heart to be again so tossed,
And from this world's adventures will withdraw.
From nothing, nothing more will I expect.
Such alchemy must contravene all sense.
Yet you by loss of all things can per-fect,
And, out of leaving, leave a permanence.
    This day I shall keep ever as a feast
    To honour one who lived love large from least.

7th May. 2003

If reprieved...

Thou knowest we must part. Though 'tis not yet,
It creeps upon us unawares, and one
Must leave; though worse to stay and not forget
The love – our times together in the sun.
Howe'er we plan, we cannot circumvent
The day, so needs must grasp the present best,
And, like poor soldiers into battle sent,
Hold all the world, save thou and I, in jest.
Dear whole of mine intent – both parts and sum.
No criticisms, whisperings that distract;
No anxiousness for anything to come;
Nor once regrets for how we've failed, or lacked.
    All is encompassed in a moment's bliss:
    And, if reprieved, why then, another kiss.

April, 2005

Today is your birthday....

for Philippa

Today is your birthday, and you say
That nothing in your life achieves success.
My old friend Hamlet nods: 'That feeling, yes,
I know it well.'
                    You snort: 'That's just a play!'
Not 'just'. The glass of fashion...moulds of form
Are aids for us to get our bearings by.
A lodestone does not glitter, catch the eye,
But helps when one is lost, or in a storm.
Of course, one wants to dare and take the chance,
But lesser actors seize the centre stage.
You'll find that message here. From every page
Peep happy-failures and irrelevance.
    'Ripeness is all.' Hold on, and live your worth.
    And mark with us, in fun, your day of birth.

14th January, 2010

Seraphim

Late-autumn men, vouchsafed by Chance or Fate,
Watch harvests gathered and the labourers too;
For them is nothing else to do but wait,
Rehearse tall tales, and fabricate them new.
In that reflective pause and interim
They learn the bitterest secret of old age:
That who were really radiant seraphim
They hurried past; or heedless turned the page.
Now, sitting by my bee-house hum gives scope
To weigh those blessings that are lost for good...
For 'bad' I'd rather say, for now there is no hope
That they will come again, or ever could.
    Yet in the knowing of the worth that's lost
    There is a gain – but at an awful cost.

28th July. 2010

Northwest Passage

All around, the ice floes bicker and groan,
Nidge and nudge strangely to the moon's long heave.
Dark leats, rhines – spread, connect, and cleave
Asunder this once hummocked Arctic zone,
Predictable to seal, and the white bear.
Six months of polar day, and six of night
When airy curtains swirl with fairy light
Were their habitual patterns of the year.
For me a sea-change, too; Age's blast of doubt.
White certainties give way. On coins of ice
Diminishing, marooned the bears and I face
Each other as our habitat runs out.
    Is this my Northwest passage through Old Space?
    Or way to rich Cathay and Isles of Spice?

29th September 2010

The Finer Gift

for Roger Watkins

You read my poems with such care, ev'n took
To show your brother. 'Larkin, Motion…who?'
You queried with a wicked tease. The book
You'd colour-coded, tagged. Its scenes you knew…
In part; where once together we have strolled
In heart and mind, as well as Adelstrop
Itself. My history kindly you unfold,
Renew its breath; and urge me not to stop.
I would that such a book, tucked in your pocket,
Well-thumbed, well-glossed with recognition's nudge,
Might – as Romances tell – stay Life's stray bullet,
Not by its value – having none to judge –
    Save that of being yours, right there and then;
    Witness to what we'd wish to live again.

8th May, 2011

Old Bunhill Fields

'Such stuff as dreams are made on'

Ariel beads of light mark out the flight
Of bees who ferry through an arc of air
Against backdrop of wall, dark buddleia
And holly bush. Each one my tricksy sprite.
Do they gather in themselves candescence,
Like pollen, luminous? Or generate
A white-dream shining from their earth-born state,
Though, at the hive, assume again substance?
Distant their flight, yet I see each distinct,
Homing against the evening fade of sky,
Or else scintilla flash on darkness winked –
'Things in motion sooner catch the eye'
    As here in Bunhill Fields' Old Cemetery.
    Good spot for spirits…and an apiary.

11th May, 2012

Bus Stop Wait

Missing…just, a bus no longer counts as loss,
Or discomposure. One can stand and wait;
Watch, idly, urgency that cuts across.
Time does not count; there is no soon or late.
Polonius' advice without the itch
To interfere; nor borrower nor lender
Be. No responsibility for any hitch;
No queue, no rank, no shopping list agenda.
There's Love, of course. With age that goes unsung;
Or else, accounted old man's foolishness.
Most feelings best to hide; few to confess.
Smirk though they will, my withers are unwrung.
    Such distancing affords me quiet solace
    As creeps that bus…destined…'Necropolis'.

1st July, 2012

Low Roofs

My parents' home

Here, in this magic circle as I stand,
I conjure Parts to re-conform, and make
One longed-for Whole – that Never-Never Land,
Once Really-Was, and dear for your dear sake.
Dawn-light whelms green from summers you have seen,
Where vine-fringe, jasmine, roses intervene;
Through hawthorn where the great pine grew; and weaves
With tiger-stripes the water-iris leaves.
Prospero-like, my island spells I plot
Of every sight and sound: th'insistent sigh
Of collared dove; while from each vantage spot,
And chimney pot, my gulls cajoling cry.
    Charms work half my wish, but never win it:
    They gain that world, but not the people in it.

25th July, 2012

Last of the Summer Wine

for Rosemary and George Pitman, John Davison, and my Liz

We walk each June; so for eleven years.
We five: two wives; schoolmasters long retired,
Whom youthful spirit, if not body, stirs
To seek by indirections if was fired –
So long ago – some beacon blaze; whom taught;
Who held a breach, came bravely off; the fun;
The failure; argy-bargy, wit. Our thought:
T'endorse a past that yet again we'd run.
In modern ways inept; not bad on maps.
With scraps of quaint allusion, knap-sacks packed,
The Downs, the Chiltern paths, Tess's mishaps
From Flintcombe-under-Ash – all these have tracked.
    Now, last of summer wine, our modern farce –
    G & T, home-based excursions, and bus pass.

3rd August. 2012

Perseids

This day would have been my mother's hundredth birthday.

'You slept soundly,' said Liz, 'right through the night.'
It was not so. Outdoors, in my pyjamas,
Stone cold to my bare feet, I looked for stars –
For Perseid showers of streaking light.
Nothing. The Northchurch clock struck four. Time passed.
Nothing. Of myself I was not aware,
Save what I wanted, and the sky was clear:
Gold points against deep velvet black contrast.
I felt I had been failed, and what desired
This night – this special night – had been denied.
Nine years ago I watched by your bedside,
Nor through that darkness then was my star fired.
    No sign. Perhaps calm Beauty must suffice –
    Expectancy, the sky tonight…your face.

12th August, 2012

Written during a Bout of Toothache

for Angie Hodges

Angels are male of sex. Well…always were
Until Victorian Burne-Jones gave them a
Hermaphrodity, bosomy, white-nightie
Appearance, which has stuck. That's alrighty
By me, I admit. A manly 'Fear not'
Is all very well when the going gets hot
Or one is gazing in the great abyss.
But I need something more than this,
And at my age the female's hard to bag.
Not (naughty thought!) King David's Abishag,
But lovely other-self who knows the score;
Will guard my back, but not lay down the law.
    Nice to have a protecting male umbrella,
    But I'll stick with my red-haired – Ἀγγελά.

14th Aug 2012

'The Old Shades', Whitehall

I came with Brian and his tank comrades
Once: an England match, oh, fifty years ago.
Guy Cunyngham drove his sporty car. 'I know
A place,' he said, '…down Whitehall…"The Old Shades".'
Quite where? Uncertain in the dark, he slewed
The tracks, and brought his sights to bear.
To park, then, – car or tank – no hard affair.
Then at the bar with beer in hand, they chewed
Old times. I loved their roaring-honest tales,
Their willingness to clasp me in. I see
Them still amid old prints, mahogany,
As now I drink with grandsons – Will and Charles.
    'The staircase to the lavatory is sudden steep,'
    I say. 'Take care if drunk or half asleep.'

18th August, 2012

Touch

Of all our senses **Touch** is Cinderella –
Before-dawn dutiful to late at night,
A modest, undemanding ancilla.
Not so, her courtly sisters: **Hearing, Sight,**
On whom we wait with care and running haste
Though often they deny their legacy.
Like muslin maiden aunts waft **Smell** and **Taste** –
Peripheral; bestowing flowers and tea.
But **Touch** at midnight leaves a slipper clue.
However slighted, shabby in old age,
She may, on instant, turn the lover's page
Back, reclaim that thrill, when one was more than two.
    My sweet Remembrancer that nothing hinders;
    Sans teeth, eyes, taste – but **never** you, dear Cinders.

19th August, 2012

The Drones

Late summer days…last chance to laze and drift
A t ease amid the ooze of honey-glow;
No urgencies of sex.
                    Then – sudden shift:
Once playmates of the month, we're now de trop.
Birth deals to us an unconvincing hand:
For work unapt, defenceless, bumbling, male.
One chosen fit Olympic stud to stand.
The rest? – mere Elvis Presleys for morale.
Now, teatime comes: we're hustled by the scruff
Returning from our constitutional!
Our women hiss: 'That's it, we've had enough;
You shan't come in – **not never more…at all.**'
    Bit bloody disappointing! Life's a hoax.
    August. We crawl away to die – just blokes.

23rd August, 2012

Lament for Lost Marmalade

For mornings of well-being, Marmalade
Is key. If any would the day enjoy
He should forswear Conserves that masquerade –
The surrogate, sham, not 'real McCoy':
Thin, gelatinous, jelly-baby flab
Not ripened on some hillside amarilla.
That never felt the sun's hot stab;
Was not, in fact, naranjas de Sevilla.
But I, with peel entire and fruit, am deft
To make enough to last through all the year.
One jar per week. A few, perhaps, to spare.
Now August's here. What!…only seven left!
    Have I misjudged? Pots stolen, or mislaid?
    Thus life runs out…Too little Marmalade!

25th August, 2012

Diary, 2012

Thirteen annual diaries on the shelf;
Three feet of space. Heav'n knows the reason why!
Do I wish to tell the world about myself?
Or agitate by proof just how times fly?
Longer mine, and more in years than Pepys.
Now, there's a thought! But how do they compare?
I'm not Chief Admiralty Clerk with heaps
Of friends, or in delicto with the odd affair.
Ink-stained incentives all elude me quite.
Challenge? Well, yes – it's easier not to write.
Perhaps one day I'll need proof I exist;
Perhaps will gather gleanings I have missed.
    And will they want to know – who follow after –
    My stock-taking of puzzlement and laughter?

1st September, 2012

On Cathy's 50th Birthday

Today I give away the dearest thing
I own; not as a careless trifle tossed,
But backward glancing, over-shouldering
At fifty years of country we have crossed.
A lock of hair, my mother-link; amulet
To ward against grey care, despair; bequeath
A joyous resilience of spirit –
Th'assured 'All will be well' that she would breathe.

While recognised, such gifts hold potency
To bulwark us with courage gone before.
The link of lock and lady is the poetry;
Forgotten once…no magic can restore.
    The provenance of love makes rich and rare;
    Without…t'would be an unknown lock of hair.

10th September, 2012

Conscious that elsewhere...

She lies in bed. Her side. Their eyes don't meet.
In the mirror she sad-eyes his clumsiness
Undressing, aware of…her clothes folded neat
Upon the chair; his male, domestic mess.
Conscious that elsewhere his glances go
Than to her, she is hurt; but to say so
Would make her vulnerable, would concede
A need; invite a response that would lead
Nowhere. She fidgets close the sheets; anxieties
Snuggle into the sleeping-bag of her mind:
Grandchildren; somewhere…Aches, Age, Perplexities.
Unstirred by single zest she lies resigned –
     Not now to England; that's past and done
     In saecula saeculorum. The sands run.

20th September, 2012

Darby and Joan

He looks away from her; something has gone,
Dried up. What…is hard to say. An absence….
Not of love. **That** moulds itself to subsidence
Like beams unseasoned in an ancient barn.
Time-honoured loyalties remain complete,
And care. But now…no animating wants,
No edge of instinct, hungering response
Or syncopation of a dance-hall beat.
Instead shoe-shuffle slow down the Eastbourne Prom.
Past the 'Best Western' and 'The Devonshire'.
He, desiccated with a dull desire;
She, drained by years of housework martyrdom.
     He knows she watches too, deducing so
     What she no longer has a wish to know.

22nd September, 2012

We'll visit together
Those places that once we visited'

'Why then latterly did we not speak?'
So Hardy asks. The answer's qualified
By silence, too. Unspoken truth is bleak
Cartography – each seeming route denied.
Once… words de trop; one knew then what was true.
Our faces, hands were passports. No small print.
But now, to read the front of Age, we screw
Our eyes, and for clues scrutable we squint;
Frame formal words to crack Quiet's carapace.
My 'How are you?' is not an idle quiz,
But foot wedged in a door I long to prise.
A grudging: '..K, alright!' will not suffice.
    The moment passes; a thousand more sneak
    Past, until the question is not asked.
                        'So Speak.'

October, 2012

Sufficient unto the day….

Forwards some people; others backwards strive.
The former briskly cross each new morn's mat;
At night put out the newspaper and cat.
Account closed. Tomorrow – next objective!
The latter – rapt in retrospective
Gaze – daisy-chain the minutes left behind,
Turn known stones, hear echoes in the wind,
And with a diary make dead days re-live.
In my mind's eye three generations go:
My children race ahead; my parents follow
Slow. I walk alone, between, in No-
-man's-land, irresolute. But now I **know**.
    We all have predilection for a tense.
    Me? oh, an Aorist man…in ev'ry sense.

18th October 2012

In Praise of Bristly Things

On hearing that Anita Björk had died

Across the trampled prairies of my sky
The vapour trails dissolve – no rack behind;
Air – stirred by messages unheard – wafts by.
All might-have-beens; not easily defined.
Yet on the bristles of my stockade-briars
Are snagged blown intimations of elsewhere:
Signed paper scraps, gold autumn's leafy fliers,
The shreds of some old coat, a strand of hair.
Praise roughnesses that catch the sleeve and stay.
Make pause, remember; gather up the thread.
A letter lies beside my hand. This day
The she who wrote so cheerily, is dead.
    One burr to another clings, barbed clues criss-cross;
    Teasel-tagged thistle-down may half cheat loss.

25th October, 2012

The Hedge

*About 1986, the skeletons of a girl and her babe were
found in the heart of a hedge near Incents, my home.*

Not a night-lodging you would have chosen:
No choice for you but snow in sleeting blasts;
Valley-wind pitiless, the ground frozen.
A maid, her babe. No trace or track. Outcasts –
No trudging on or back. Here at the edge
Of Goose Field, from Grub Lane, you crouch,
Kneel…feel…into the twig-spiky deep hedge –
No shieling shelter. Your numbed fingers touch
The fold in the thin shawl. Not far…tavern-
Haven warmth; Rectory. Would they reprove
The plight of a girl, the cry of a bairn?
Matters not now. 'Shsh, my sweeting, my love.'
    Two…three…hundred winters have turned that page.
    I have loved you now for more years than your age.

21st May, 2013

'The skies are painted with unnumbered sparks'
Julius Caesar

The stars and planets in my primaeval
Youth were a comforting personal
Presence; 'bright officious lamps', but more –
Old friends and myths. Bright holes in Heaven's floor
By heroes cut – their final frontier.
Chaos defined by pasted cardboard cut-outs:
Orion, Pegasus, Cassiopoeia;
The Plough for navigators and Boy Scouts.
Our sky – a patterned duvet laid with love.
Now, though, we know but barrenness of space;
Dark matter by Mechanics kept in place
And impetus of some cold Big-Bang shove.
    But when I see a gorgeous shooting star
    I re-flect how skies **were**…less how they **are.**

24th August, 2013

43, St Anne's Road

for Brian and Dorothy Millen

'We shall be alright. We have books to read,'
Say dear souls curled in cardigan'd-neat age,
Content in each other's heedlessness of need,
And comforting predictability of page.
She sitting on the green, rough-weave settee;
He, in the Ercol chair – its arms rubbed clear
Of varnish by the sleeves of his tweed
Jacket – 'Liddell Hart' on lap, beside the fire.
How cruelly Fate removes the props; subtly
Rearranges the chess pieces on the board
When one has slipped away to make a cup of tea…
Or dozed! 'We have our books. Be re-assured!'
    Fond hope! Peek one moment from the turret,
    And fall a prey to that fell Sniper's bullet.

11th November, 2013

Zodiac Crabbing

'Yourself, sir, shall grow old as I am, if like
a crab you could go backwards.' Hamlet

A lifetime back – quite literally – we'd kneel,
Us kids, upon a sea-slimed groyne, and reel
Up pebble-weighted lines, baited with scraps
Of food, to catch, from muddy depths – the crabs.
No hooks. They'd simply cling on tight to what
They'd got, and wave 'Hallo' with claws vaunt-armed –
All angles, legs – then in the bucket plopp'd.
We always put them back, quite safe, unharmed.
At Blakeney I saw children, recently,
With 'Champion Crabber' blazoned on each shirt.

Now giant Champion Crab has reeled up…me;
Resurgo to a novel world…unhurt?
    'For old times' sake, my friend, you're honour-bound
    To see me home, and set me safe and sound.

12th November, 2013

Busted Flush

Beyond all doubt, Men…are a busted flush;
Maleness of its very nature does for us.
Our youth – one self-destructive madcap rush;
Our age – with impotence, ridiculous….
Irrelevant. Our cover story's blown:
We are – admit! – genetically flawed;
Rude cancers feed on our testosterone;
Fatherhood is out of date with semen stored;
The issue of dead Caesar brought to life.
No woman need now call herself a wife.
The obvious answer to it all is this:
The bees' response – parthenogenesis.
    Yet listen to the hive: 'Without the male…'
    Buzz female worker-bees, '…morale will fail.'

21st December, 2013

Falkland Perspective, 2013

'…would men observingly distil it out.' Henry V

For my three girls: Philippa, Nicola and Catherine

Though all the wideness of the world between,
We always knew you would be there – blood kin –
If ill-bred neighbours threatened to annex
These small and aimless empire-outpost specks;
Unlovely isles with low storm-battered shores –
Of all my years the home. You ours, we yours –
In that old-English way without emotion's fuss,
Steeped in histories that distinguish us.
Then…sudden: rude invasion; uncouth voices;
Our flag unmasted, struck my ancient choices.
Not waiting for slow logic to approve,
You sent a Task Force solely out of love.
   'My father means the world to me,' I overheard;
   Am almost glad my peace has been so stirred.

December, 2013

They Crowd in Close

They crowd in close. Those dear ones whom
I long have missed, now, even at a turn of stair
Or setting of a chair or entry to a room
Waylay me on a sudden unaware; and there…
Just there…appear; and where left off resume –
Without surprise or sighs of long regret –
The homeliness that may old love relume
In wonder of a wordless tête-à-tête.
I cannot think that I should thus be stirred
By random figuration of the air
Or casual conversation overheard,
Had they not made of me their market square.
    And if so now, then – certain – time will come
    When I shall knock, and they will be at home.

11th January, 2014

A Hundred Sonnets…

'A hundred sonnets of Old Age! If that's
Your aim, you had better get your skates on;
Watch out for Marvell's "wingéd chariots" –
Not when…not how; but, simply, Termination.'
This No-man's-land in Time defines the task.
So much to do; my nuts-and-bolts agenda.
'Does any of it matter?' you may ask.
Don't listen, Pearce; bash on, and no surrender.
Ideas rifle at me in the night;
Are lost like tracer arcing through the dark.
The goal I longed for may be out of sight;
Too late for sonnets that might cut a mark,
    But never out of place…a crisp salute.
    'Go, dear Horatio, bid the soldiers shoot.'

13th January, 2014

Metamorphosis

'Sweet are the uses of adversity,'
So sang the hamadryad in the oak.
'Though rooted in one spot, my spirit's free;
Here host am I to all the fairy folk;
A magic tree that sighing lovers mark
Who make their trysts beneath my shade
Carving their names, love symbols, in my bark.
And hanging tokens round my elfin glade
Which shift in airs, and catch the light, and say:
Nothing of harm, unseemly here, or tears.
Just calm content – summation of the years.
J 'y suis, j'y reste; so with each guest, I stay.
　　Such entertainment could there never be
　　Had I not been transfigured to a tree.'

14th January, 2014

Little Gidding, 1
The Gifts reserved for Age

'
'Cold friction of expiring sense…
As body and soul begin to fall asunder'

'Cold friction of expiring sense' makes Age
Review its crabbed, slow sunderings from Youth.
We clamber back, dislodging every stage,
Each once-discovery of newfoundland truth,
And each is 'seemly', 'comely' – Old English words
That still do duty through our years and tears –
Like pictograms, re-pieced, on ancient sherds
Telling of Pharoah's charioteers.
The trauma of now-losing's never new.
To prospect-shore from river-shallow –
The narrow cot, the gatherings by the yew:
To come, to go – the difference is the arrow.
　　So winter squirrels frisk for mislaid plunder
　　Heedless of Mr Eliot's 'asunder'.

30th January, 2014
Charles, King and Martyr

Little Gidding, 2

'...*rage*
At human folly, and the laceration
Of laughter at what ceases to amuse'

A character in 'ITMA' used to say:
'What's funny in that?' in the Midland-dull
Accent of a ventriloquist's doll.
Dad and I mimicked his naïveté.
But now, what's 'funny' has the manic whiff
Of mindless, speaker-amplified, guffaws.
Not bravo-stirring genuine applause,
But lemming laughter, heading for the cliff.
'Those whom the gods wish to destroy' – the fable
Tells – 'they first make mad' – 'dementant prius',
Must make us ponder how the stark gods see us,
And if they are to blame for all our Babel.
    But Eliot is wrong: the old don't 'rage';
    Just watch with sad, sad helplessness of Age.

February, 2014

Little Gidding, 3

The Gifts reserved for Age

'The rending pain of re-enactment
Of all that you have done'

Were my record: 'Crimes grievous and abhorred',
I might stand nobly in the dock. 'Prisoner,
Have you anything to say?' 'Nothing m'lord.'
And worn two shirts so not be seen to shiver.
But mine – a mean, unthink-unthanking blame.
Venial. Taking for granted gifts of love.
All little infelicities of shame
That, fasting, Lent's remorse may not remove.
For such – in Uttoxeter's market-square –
Sam Johnson paid his penance in the rain.
We practise merit not in what we do,
But how we would do, came the chance again.
  I used to say, 'There must be no regret.'
  'Nothing m'lord' sounds glib in retrospect.

Ash Wednesday, 18th February, 2015

Not from self-interest quite….

I sit on the floor by the fireside, one
Arm across your knee. Why is it that we
Who have loved each other, shared, shown and known
For twice eleven thousand days, should be
Loath to confide some last least moiety?
Would trust with cheque-book, tablets, life; rely
For diary-prompting, doctors, toast and tea;
Yet at that narrow water-jump we shy?
We fudge th'uncertainties that lie ahead;
Deny that loneliness is more, but courage lesser:
Not from self-interest quite, but slippered dread
That we are shamed. Yet to a confessor,
    Lover, stranger even – who cannot call
    Us to accompt, we merrily blurt all.

January 2014

Red Letter Day

This day… is Feast of Ermengild, Princess
Of Kent; Abbess of Ely, and of Minster.
A saint of seabird calls, of watery loneliness,
Great wimpling winds. But few have heard of her.
In that great ship that rides the Fens her bones
Are borne unknown. She has no cult; no worshippers –
Save two. The heavenly switchboard phones
For her are quiet, and few the e-mail prayers.
'Excuse me, E..R …Would that be Ermengytha
You want, or Erminold? Ah, Ermengild!
I'll put you straight through. You'll soon be with her.
Take care! May your petitions be fulfilled.'
    So, we have hot-line action in a trice;
    A guardian saint's attention – which is nice!

13th February, 2014

Tiresias

I, Tiresias communicant with gods;
Party to their feuds; sought as a seer,
Live as on a threshold where each pauser nods –
The in-between. No kinship anywhere.
That neither-way when the boat's keel
Circles in 'choros' round the anchor chain;
Unmoving centre of the spinning wheel.
Nor Male nor Female; Old…made Young again
By Zeus; Blinded by Hera, but by bird-
Song become a Sighted hearer; Slighted
Yet Revered; Unheeded, though I speak Truth's word
To Oedipus – why his reign is blighted.
   The sweats come on; I sit below Thebes walls –
   Tiresias…with shrivelled dugs…and shrunken balls.

10th February, 2014

'I thought I was going to lose you at Christmas'

A plume of smoke hangs always over Etna.
The giant sleeps.
                'We know. Our soil is rich;
Our vines grow strong; danger is a familiar
Creature. We laugh and quaff, and we forget the risk.'

That, for the artist, completes the picture:
The frisson of calamity that lurks
Behind the arras. Under ground. The whisper
Of our nature – fragile to such quirks.

I love the light and dark, the never dull,
The intimacy of sunshine with the storm,
The 'just-you-wait-and-see', the sudden thrill.
One lives with each; each seems awhile the norm.
   Yet, just one caveat I'd like to urge:
   Not, please **not today**, the pyroclastic surge.

21st February, 2014

Letter

Dear Keats, thank you for yours of the 16th ult.
The English spring! yes, oh, yes, beyond a doubt.
Today I realised, with a sudden jolt,
It is St David; daffodillies out;
Coy snowdrops, primroses; the crocuses
A purple flare in Sidmouth gardens here;
Quadrille of insects in the sun, while bees
'Expatiate'; with gusto drill the air.
Such garnerings we cram into our scrip –
Prescription for your 'Capability'!
Though most would argue the futility
When that fell Sergeant holds us in his grip –
    You and I discard the irritable 'Why?'
      To hug dear Beauty through this year's Goodbye.
              Ever yours sincerely,   James Rice

St David's Day, 2014

James Rice and Keats were friends. Neither had good health and both died young (Keats in 1821; Rice in 1832). Rice liked to convalesce in Sidmouth. It was to him that Keats wrote from Wentworth Place, Hampstead, about wanting to see again the simple flowers of spring. In September, 1820, he set sail for Italy, never to return.

14th August, 1956 or 1957

for Darling Liz

So many aunts inhabited my youth –
Some self-appointed; all seemed very old.
I hardly knew them if the truth be told,
But all expected to be kissed. Averse
To this and shy; nursed on 'Ivanhoe', Conan
Doyle, Tennyson – high Romance occupied
My knightly scene; therein no woman
Freely kissed but that she be my ever-bride.

None knew that resolution of great weight,
And so – 'You never kiss me; why?' one said.
For just that 'Why', I celebrate this date;
That moment – **then** – our whole life's course decided.
    Now, three-score years…near on, I've kept my word.
    How happy I have been. You think absurd?

St David's Day, 2014

Departure

From a carriage window I lean; intent…
(Think: Troops on film entraining for the Front)
…on you, my flagged pavilion from the world.
'Cheery' is always the cheating, hackneyed word;
And 'bravely' you, as women always do,
Must let me go. Doors bang, the whistles blow.
The moment, even now, is slipping,
Seeping, through our hands. 'Finger-tipping' –
Nothing else is. We two; entire of us; all time
In this one touch; 'For ever, you are mine'.
I match a line against a platform sign…
Verticals – and fear to see them dis-align
    The wheels nudge. Reality retreats in a blur
    Of tears and speed – redeemed by you for ever.

2nd March, 2014

'There is figures in all things'
Welsh Fluellen

'Gainst the east window that pours brimmed flagons
Of light across the altar, flap tortoiseshells,
Trapped. A killing-jar; wire-mesh beyond.
And, up and up, among the traceried curls
And cusps stir more: **eight** altogether…
Hazed in incense smoke, in atomies of dust,
Struggling to attain where they have never
Been. Church-hatched, despatched; short shrift between.
                                                    Just
Then, to prove some point, one settles on my sleeve;
'Earth-colouring attracts,' a friend nearby
Says. It seems at home, and loath to leave;
Intent on sharing secrets ere it die.
    To the mediaeval mind…an allegory;
    Fluellen would concur. **Eight years?** We'll see.

15th March, 2014

Buying Time

Buying Time in age is waste of time; and hope.
It is mere buying days. And days are days
Wherein one only begs for more, though scope
To fill their store is vain down future ways;
Trading for nought those restless thoughts that pound
At night with radiant beings, glories spun…
For penny-packet pills, and sleep. Th'old hound
Shifts stiffly in the window-square of sun.
The usurer grinds interest from the principal;
The pawnbroker sells what cannot be redeemed.
Even so, Time solicits our approval
Then cancels promises that can be only dreamed.
    Better to hear the horn sound 'Gone Away',
    And leave with 'Tally ho'…to bright new day.

17th April, 2014

Towards Burrow Mump

This was a sedgy, water-edgy place of fog
Once, where hazels, axe-hacked into track,
Sprang back, and causeways rifted into gurgling bog.
Directions explicit only by their lack.
No firmness…only in resolve to wade
And wallow further; slip, slide, slash and splash;
Observing bird sky-ways through osier braid;
The slope of sun through willow wand and ash.

The lines of lane and rhine may, even now, confuse
All but the eel and otter, marsh-bred fowler.
A land of ancient crafts and mystic clues,
Of legends, and alignments of earth power.
    Today, I fix my course on one strange hill
      That, rising from the floods, seems out of place, unreal.

24th April, 2014

On Burrow Mump

To this unlikely hill my steps are bent:
Mump Hill – lone cone upon a flood-plain plate.
Will climbing up be by the steep ascent,
Like Bunyan's emblem of the narrow gate?
Or like Donne's hill where Truth by turns is found,
And turn about; and one may pause upon the way
To catch one's breath, admire the view far round,
Debate a point, and watch the lambs at play?

This magic summit gives my journey bearing;
Is pattern to past-being and new-finding;
My summer's set of seeing; scratched-stone caring.
This ruined tower, Time's gnomon of reminding.
    The spirits join me on this hill's skied crown.
    Then, hand-held loving, helter-skelter…down.

24th April, 2014

Restlessness

Put out the light, and then…? Nothing avails:
Potations, pills, hot baths, sleep therapies
I've tried the lot. A million maggoty snails
Crawl over flesh; sirens blare; my mind is
A squad-car chasing down impossible rhymes,
All law-abiding traffic jams; is shoved
To the kerb. Three a.m. The worst of times.
'Keep young and beautiful if you want to be loved.'
The silly, taunting lyric will not go away.
Songs are for the young, who will never learn.
Why did we never learn, and seize the day?
And I remember – as I toss and turn –
　　The peace and stillness of long-ago rest,
　　One Provençal night…my head on your breast.

April, 2014

An Afternoon at Aller

for A.J.H.

Thou art not perfect, love, no more am I;
Foolish our thoughts if we regard us so,
Nor should we come at happiness thereby,
Nor find a need for soil where we may grow;
But sigh, with pale content, in orbits where we glide.
Each, the glowworm glimmer of a single star;
Then, fretful lest one day we might collide
And lose identity of what we think we are.

But out of two, as one, we draw all gaze:
The tango tosses and the duet plays;
Our syncopated pattern wins the praise,
And in the stars' conjunction is the blaze.
　　At Aller, our bells different in their sounds
　　Tongue side by side, and so complete the rounds.

1st May, 2014

'Oh! the difference...'

In a performance of 'King Lear'

It was a torrid clinch, mouth hard on lips;
Clasping of buttocks.
                              Enter Albany.
Hurried rearrangements: Goneril zips
Tight, decently, her skirt from hip to knee;
And: 'Oh! the difference of man and...**man**'
She hisses with a pointed emphasis.
Eruption of laughter – 'Know what you mean'.
Such observations Girls-together do not miss.
For just a moment my fancies wander
To the audience, and how these women weigh
The worthy dull against the spry philanderer.
Hard is to hit which one will win the day.
     In any wooing, though – affairs of heart,
     'Yours in the ranks of Death' seems a good start.

4th May, 2014

Of course there is a God...

Of course there is a God – whether Him or Her.
No random cosmic force, gravity, or gene
Could so exquisite be in timing's torture,
So personal in disregard or spleen.
We are created only to be frustrated.
'As flies to wanton boys'...toy soldiers rather,
For God controls all armies; all are fated
In the playroom trenches – to the canned laughter
Of the television. We are shown glories,
But they are snatched. Given Youth with impatience;
Wisdom in Old Age, but none to heed our stories.
The pension comes with wheelchair and incontinence.
     Of course there is a God, and I am vexed.
     'All's right!' you think?
                              'Just see what happens next.'

13th May, 2014

The Fourth Temptation

'Sorry to disturb, dear Man. It's me again.
Not a temptation this; a comment more.
That silly tack: "**My** Kingdom; **You** can reign"
Was utterly inept. For you, I'm sure…last straw.
Come with me – I do so want to be of use –
Two thousand years down Time with Doctor Who.
Your message still resounds; they've no excuse.
Yet…wars, abuse …abound. Nothing is new.
You've tried, but what's the point? I'd jack it in
If I were you. Beg pardon… "Fuck the lot"
I'd say, and settle down with that nice Magdalen.'

'That's just the point, you see. Not **me**…you're not.
   If you, Old Grudge, did not induce Despair
   All this would change; and you the happier.'

May, 2014

To a Child watching my Bees

Sit close beside, this late June afternoon,
And **watch** my whiffling harvesters arrive;
How courteously they rendez-vous, commune,
And wait their turn when laden to the hive.
Shout 'Pollen' as the padding workers hump
Their leggy bundles, orange, red and grey.
And **look!** – a lumpen drone lands…bump
Upon his sisters, who shrug as if to say:
'You're male; we're busy; don't get in our way
While we enquire of sisters coming in
The whereabouts of some gold-rich Cathay,
Then haste to fill our larder to the brim.'
   'Busy as bees'…from dawn to last of light.
   Mind how you go. Oh, no!
         Avoid the line of flight!

24th June, 2014

At the Garden's End

It's evening now: rose petals flake the lawn
Where the crab tree shades. Four swifts doh-see-doh
Against pink glimmered clouds. The breeze has drawn
Round to the west. Still urgent, to and fro,
The bees…each aura'd with light's ghosty spill;
Their murmur merging to the dragon roar
Within. Such din of masons, like the teeming will
Of stadium or forge. From that dark store
Oozes a not-yet honey scent – sweet, heavy,
Ripe – attracting wasp marauding roughs
Gainst whom, come wet or fine, the guarding levy
Holds the line, tight-wedged; and 'St-e-ady, now, the Buffs'.
    So night comes on apace, and the bat flits.
    And here, with many thousand friends, DRAP sits.

24th June, 2014

Downsizing

A Kingsize bed is where they live a-night.
Not the great Bed of Ware, but it would sleep
Five or six intimates if packed in tight;
Though rest be hardly undisturbed or deep.
For them horizons now have shrunk like Donne's
To the bed's foot. Each claims a bedside ledge;
Between them…Terra Incognita…Dragons.
Each lone co-partner of an ancient pledge
Inhabits…somewhere space. Once was they dealt
Such excitation as moved all who saw.
Believe it yet – 'Let Rome in Tiber melt' –
For they, forgetful, dream their own folklore.
    Memo: downsize one's bed; let assets all depart;
    But yield up – never – kingdoms of the heart.

29th June, 2014

Recessions

List! **Four** Recessions from Reality.

My father spoke of Age's bittersweet:
Wisdom to see; not power to remedy
Life's ills. The Past more real. The **first** Retreat.

Malfunction, next, of body; loss of strength;
The step falls short; though, still, will to compete.

The **third** – perceived strange change of focal length
Between oneself and objects one might greet.
It's not that one no longer cares, but that
Care has no point; no flutter of heartbeat;
Response is dulled; the print-out graph near flat.

And so – to almost last – the **fourth** Retreat.
 Bird-eerie cries from…hush…enshrouding mist;
 Grey leaf and prow in seeming stasis. List!

July, 2014

The Fifth Temptation, 1

Cattura di Cristo nell' orto

'And Satan entered into Judas who was called Iscariot'

Judas speaks:

Now, **this**, the picture that I wish to show;
That gets, I say, beneath the skin of life,
By that old villain, Caravaggio –
Familiar with paint brush as with knife.
Night-brawling scenes no novelty. See, Judas' face
Older, fleshy, furrowed in perplexity,
And his tormented tokened, taut embrace.
Betrayal ! No, not easy…not for him…er…me.
You knew…You knew…**yet** let me go ahead.
Such calm acceptance… 'Christlike', all agree.
Without **me**, though, your life untold, unread.
I hauled you into living history.
   The artist clasps your destiny to mine:
   Both of us…Big Time…in the Grand Design.

9th July, 2014

The Fifth Temptation, 2

My words must prompt you to a note of pique
And Pentateuch rebuke. But I am bound
To **question**. Caravaggio's technique
Does just that in a way that is profound.
That knack he has…skewers the viewer's gaze,
And forces him by colour-contrast, line,
To the one point-in-time he must appraise.
Those faces leap…three – yours, and John's, and mine
(Judas', I mean) …from the convened design;
From triangles of hands, and arms, armour.
Why? Because white needs black to make it shine.
Flesh…night…steel. Chiaroscuro, drama.
   Your drama is made luminous by me.
   'Amazing,' all say, 'that…serenity !'

~ ~ ~

I don't presume a kiss for all I've done,
But to shake hands were sporting, God's Own Son.

9th July, 2014

Just Checking

By my hives I sit…dozing…day-dreaming…
In the warmth; mind lost in space, in suspense;
Eyes an open lens etching bees streaming
By a backdrop of lavender, and fence;
An articulated streak of joined-up dots;
Or tracer rearing up, certain to strike,
Then, veering away: A medley of motes.
And…(nearer my thoughts this day)…they are like
The EC-graph that has graved the drum beat
Of my heart in a headlong steepling urge
To go on till the music is complete –
As these who hummingly…con-verge, di-verge.
    Now, summer's hectic pace has slackened.
    All is well. July, garnered…at an end.

31st July, 2014.

Not just about War

*'Have you heard of nothing strange about the streets? …
'Tis the god Hercules.'*
                'Antony and Cleopatra'

Night. As I walk, the century is unwound.
The filed or lonely dead await their turns;
Waiting…deep hush; what weight of dark! What sound?
Here…there, a window where a candle burns.
All over Europe, **then**, *the lamps were going out.*
Millions dimly stir, muster, prepare;
The distant tuck of drum; wings brush the air.
One way, one way, the nation drills to Doubt.

How real is Fancy! Lying side by side,
Now, lost in thought, we know that never before
For us has movement been one way: no turn of tide;
No prospect of re-turn. This is the day of War.
    The theme has changed. Not: 'It will always be
    The other man'…but, now: **'That man is me.'**

3rd August, 2014

10 p.m., August 4th

Late evening. One hour to go…to…something …
Not breath 'd. Wings brush air, soundlessly. I know –
As I draw by – that these browed houses watching…
Know, tuned to History. One hour to go.
The die, once cast, is History; the cards fall
One way for the gypsy woman to read.
In windows, candles mourn what must befall.
Not even gods can change a Fate decreed.
Late, and hourly older, on raw duck-boards
Of unrest, I prove, dear Love, the lesson
That Movement, through Time, seeps only **Towards.**
One way. No further chance. No return.
    From: 'Always will be the other man', the text
    Has been revised to: 'It is my turn – next.'.

4th August, 2014

Super Moon

for my sister, Margaret, on our mother's 102nd birthday

I would have tracked you right across the sky
Last night, but some prose flimflam came between.
Sleep…curvature of earth…remorse deny
A steady utterness to all-has-been;
A 'Super Moon'; a dazzling glory show
Approaching nearer than for many a year.
My sister caught her breath in Greek Nimborio,
Far off; and yet in wonder we concur.

This night was Moon entire. Nothing else was;
As if all radiance and love had once,
Unthanked, been mine; familiar to clasp –
And not again shall come that lovely chance.
    When I awoke I knew that all was gone,
    And, now, make-do with greater-lesser sun.

10th August, 2014

It Suited Me

Wherewith my mother dressed me as a boy,
Regretfully, that body I must slough.
Flesh-uniform of collar, shirt and cuff
Empowering me with urgent, carefree joy
From that birth when I de-camped from her
Long since, who was my nine months' fitting glove.
When, careful stitching of a mother's love,
The new-print pattern of a father's measure,
Lent me this hand-down of the family;
Comfortable to former wearing; styled
Conformable to mine. **It suited me!**
Now, though…by cancer's sweat-shop-trade defiled.
    In happy hijinks many a year
    I sported loaned and manly vestiture.

September 2014

With One Big Breath

Candles…not this year…no…shall I blow out,
But let them blaze, however long they take;
Shielding their flames from ev'ry flickering doubt,
And hand them twinkling with each slice of cake.
Today's my time for giving **out** (not **up**)
Presents to all of whom I so approve;
Who merrily with me have drained life's cup,
Then old; now young, who hold me in their love.
So, no more thought of snuffing out the flames
With one big breath, or more – or wheezy none;
No one may leave before the party games;
My seven-seventh year has just begun.
    Grandma's Footsteps may creep…stop short…then jog,
    But this is not, as yet, the epilogue.

23rd September, 2014

Routes

for Stephen

Spread out the map – Land's End to John 'o Groats –
To plot my cycling journeys past, where tyres
From hub and homely haven took these routes
Un-known – here look like telegraphic wires.

Their humming messages still may be scanned.

If ever **you** should think to be a darer
And share in risk – with resting place unplanned –
The chancy triumphs of the wayfarer;
To shout aloud wild snatches on the long hill
Down; be doggéd upward when the long hill stays;
To measure miles with thanks for what they will,
Then know that I am there before; my gaze
   On finger post, on bridge, next hilly top,
   And wayside inn…though seldom time to stop.

28th September, 2014

'The Street', Whitstable

Pocked limpet rocks and puddingstone; concrete
Debris of the 'Invasion' scare; starfish
Stiff orange-fingered in the shallow wash –
Are my boyhood remembrance of 'The Street',
Which at low tide thumbs out a mile to meet
The sunsets firing over Sheppey hills.
Rockpools used to bait a refugee retreat
For shrimps and sidelong crabs from herring gulls,
While sun-black, blistered wrack invaded
Slum condominiums of mussel shells.
In shallows, in old paddlers we waded
Deep in slimey mud with lug-worm whorls.
   Sharp-eyed we'd find – where dainty turnstones flight –
   Clay pipes, and mermaid's purses…iron pyrite.

29th September, 2014

'The Street', 2

Two brief dis-mantlings by day and night
Allow 'The Street' to breathe in sun and wind,
And smell the salt-sea-tang. Then, a boy might –
Still might – like a shrewd oyster-catcher, find
Life a-plenty: crabs – not so big or many
Now; star fish, anemones which we would prod
To see them squirt; the goby and the blenny –
Rock-pool darters; gleaming cuttle bones – food
For budgerigars. A roundy whelk egg-case
Bowls in the breeze. Parachuting jelly fish
That might be scooped and thrown in splashing chase,
Left stranded in the sun, would melt and vanish.
    Kingdom of gull, and shell, seaweed and worm.
    When I wash up there, I will know I'm home.

August, 2014

'The Street', 3

One morning – wintry still and misty grey,
Waters playfully unzipping on 'The Street' –
Shoes in hand, currents tugging at bare feet,
We waded out so far where one must weigh
Tide's turn: 'Is this the end? How far the end?'
Paused – my mother and I (aged about eight);
Then beat hasty retreat, before too late
And we must swim. Almost, we were penned.
But, scamp'ring back, set land's beseiged domain
With castles moated. Quick! Hurry! Stones, shells, stack
Up, bind fast with flapping kelp and bladderwrack:
Stern bastions of conquest. All in vain.
    Marooned, each stood within the encroaching tide.
    Shore-safe, we watched them…one by one…subside.

August, 2014

Carpe Punctum Temporis

Seize the **Moment**: not the **Day.** That is too
Big, and often tows its caravan of woes:
Remorse, hankering hard upon its cue
To tag Blake's infant Joy before it grows.
The **Moment**, though, is starburst vision
That overwhelms us with its sudden flare;
The artist's deft brush-stroke precision;
The sapient word that gentles care;
The crystal shimmering of winter air;
The lover's glance that lays love bare;
The burrs that gather on rough tweed;
Comeliness exactly matching need.
    The nano-second scorch of Leonid light
    Is Memory's torch through Chaos and Old Night.

September 2014

'A box where sweets compacted lie'

So many odds and ends. What could they mean
To **him**? It's doubtful that he could explain
The provenance of each. What seen…where been.
Yet that they **did** mean much to him…is plain.
Around his study – cluttering shelf and ledge,
In cabinet, bureau, boxes – find: clay shards,
Small stones from mountain top or river's edge,
Great shells from far Malay, bright feathers, cards –
'To Dad, with love', old letters, fir cones, photos
Of whom we cannot tell for sure, fossils,
Teasels, tufts of old-man's-beard: mementoes
Of a hoarder! Oh, what disorder jostles!
    For him: 'A box where sweets compacted lie'.
    For us: black bin-bag job. 'Heigh ho,' we sigh.

9th Sept.2014

'The Sun is God'

The Artist, J. M. W. Turner

September's end: gold harvest; daily blue
The sky – sunniest since nineteen-ten we're told;
Better than any my father ever knew.
I'm watching bees, and thinking: 'Will luck hold…
Another year?' Warmth sits upon my shoulder.
Wax cells are filled; new brood is laid; bees hum
Contentment; and though the breeze hints colder,
Yet trundling ivy-pollen in…they come.
Hunger for life drives all. But there is loss:
Workers, worn out, knowing their time is done,
Clamber – they cannot fly – through ragged grass,
Doggedly lawn-length long, toward the sun;
    Driven by a purpose not fathomed quite:
    Perhaps the sun **is** God; and Turner right.

29th September, 2014

'Clebantine & Wreaths and Roses'
by Arthur Pearce

On second-hand bookshelves always are tucked
Poetry prints too thin for a title
In gold upon the spine; the which, if plucked
Forth, and read, might afford fair requital.
Crown octavo, font 'Garamond', faded, foxed;
Hobnobbing with Victorian Flora, Fauna;
For the Charity Shop, eventually boxed
In an out-of-the-way dark corner.
Once, the genteel pursuit of quaint folk
Who stirred at night and reached for paper, pen
To cope with firefly thoughts, before they woke
And settled to their breakfast world again.
    Arthur Pearce's poems – moral, pushy –
    Will never sell. Clebantine – who was she?

October, 2014

Handprint

A handprint has been discovered deep in a cave in Indonesia.
It is thought to be 40,000 years old, and the earliest
example of creativity that exists — older than similar proofs
from caves in France and Spain.

Mn creep back deep in long cold dark...air thick
un day un way...foot stone stub hand rub...drip
plink.....sshh...red clay bag slung...smoke shake flame stick...
screak...where...**Old Ones Gone Ones Bone Ones**...gut grip
hard...*huh*...ghost wings...*aah*...bang by...once moons dead
Mn held warm breast beat here...now self in dark...
own big fear thump...**Mn** self...for **Them**...now spread
hand spit...*Pthah*...hand spit...*Pthah*...**Mn** gift...one day...**mark**

Some forty thousand years since then have trod;
Yet still her breath curls in my inner space,
Honouring parents and a cryptic god.
Longing, at once, to know Will Be and Was.
   Those pianist fingers; that bird-foot span —
   More eloquent than these spat marks of mine.

9th October, 2014

The Present Participle

Matthew Arnold once was asked if he was
'Saved'. To the stranger he replied: "Do you mean
'Σεσώμενος' – saved, or 'σωζομενος' –
Being saved? A difference is between."
Never is **certain** saved, and if we were…
From what? Casual mischance, madness, loss
Of friends, cancer of the bowel, tremor
Of the Stock Exchange? Life doesn't give a toss,
My friend. And 'saved' **by** what? Some flash of light;
A lifeboat in Titanic night; prescribed salves;
Compliance with some Given Writ or Rite?

We delve salvation slowly in ourselves;
    By love that we have always known somewhere,
    Or known, by clues, it must exist…somewhere.

October, 2014

'Allone withouten anie compaignye'

'The Knight's Tale', Chaucer'

Drawing towards their evensongs – old stags,
And elephants are émigrés, alone.
Far from the muster the aged tusker lags,
Instinct to find that fabled grove of bone,
Or, failing, hanker mammoth memories back.
Victor of five trampling ruts, the antlered hart,
Broken, limps a solitary track.
Silently the captains and the kings depart,
And bees without a remonstrating buzz,
Crawl, singly, at their end away. They know.

Even so, one lights a candle without fuss,
And of Time's ill-befitting makes no show,
    But watches – as a gentleman would choose
    With handkerchief that's neat; clean, polished shoes.

October, 2014

Male Panther

A course of oestrogen injections given
to destroy cancer-feeding testosterone

A panther lived, once, deep in that dark glade.
Like Blake's tiger he was wondrous bright,
With energy to fascinate and make afraid.
Male-proud, he prowled the feral night.
If truth be told, though, he was rarely spied –
Kept wary distance from the villagers;
If ever there was rumpus he would hide.
But…stirrings in the darkness count as dangers,
And word was put around he must be killed:
'We can't be sure, and you can never tell.'
Risk was assessed; frail opposition quelled;
Witch-doctors watched the moon, and cast their spell.
   Now living safely there, a shy-eyed hind
   Knows nothing of a beast of different kind.

30th October. 2014

Ditchling Hill

The London-to-Brighton Cancer Bicycle Ride, with Nicola and William
My hi-viz tabard emblazoned with 'Port of Tyne'

The Hill reared as we neared the South Downs' line.
In mind, for days before – Ditchling! where contour
Lines bunch tight. A 'Pilgrim's Progress' metaphor.
'The Big One now' threatened a verge-side sign.
We puffed up… trudged! Some bent on cycling fame.
Help I declined; dead-beat a frequent spell,
But laughed when, slogging by, one gasped: 'Fucking Hell'.
'F…ing Hill', he might have said – it was all the same.
Around the summit post we sprawled, and viewed
Where we had come. Then…easy now the way –
Downhill. Applause. The Bright One. Zest renewed.
Collecting my medal, I heard one say:
       'There, look! "Port of Tyne!"…the old man we thought
       Would die – on Ditchling Hill.' He did in sort.

25th October, 2014

Raking Leaves

Thought-struck 'Last time! Perhaps the very last!'
Lends curious piquancy to a task.
Raking the autumn leaves as they fall fast –
A few…last cherry…still to fall – I ask
Myself if I shall ever get things spick and span
Again: a tidy shed, bee frames prepared
Before the wet sets in, and: 'Time to batten
Down', as father, always with a grin, announced.
A voice breaks in, accusing – pat on cue –
'You have **buried** the leaves, they must be **binned.'**
'O reason not the need' I mutter as I always do.
Not more sinned against, I; but having sinned!
       'And that the last time, too?' I wonder. Go
       To put away my spade and rake and hoe.

25th October, 2014

Coral Reef

I want to say…but no!…would rather not
Use **words** at all. But long that you should know
My **Mind** – an unpolluted coral grot
Where unlikely, lovely, rhythmic fish glow
Rainbow-coloured, orange, azure, peridot…
Endlessly…unhurriedly…**word**lessly:
A water world of shimmering sun-shot.

Thoughts, though, with **Words** are frequently
At odds. And **Acts**, they say, more loudly speak
Than both. Perhaps. But on my Barrier Reef
Poor Helmsman **Acts** has foundered many a barque
Which **Thought's** true charting might have brought home
safe.

I, then, had been your ideal man. No beard:
Young face. And for a beard you never cared.

1st November, 2014

Suspension of Belief

Such fun, as kids, to act out being old:
Rummaging the wardrobe; lip-stick wrinkles drawn;
Walking-stick totter; baggy trousers rolled.
Awfully good: quite to the manner born –
Which is the case. Imitation makes Age
Convincing. I had John Aubrey to a T;
I made him live. Victor Meldrew on stage
And Corporal Jones **are** our Reality.

Problem. The Agéd are unreal, lack vigour,
Are embarrassing – are 'Things which are **Not'** –
Bad teeth, incontinence, wind. Don't snigger;
Poor dears can't help it. They have lost the plot.
    Reality. For all there comes a time
    Too far to catch in make-believe or rhyme?

3rd November, 2014

Eurydice Moment

I brought you to the door to say goodbye,
But you said: 'I'll come a little further.
Night hides tears; I'd not be seen to cry.'
So hand in hand, and wordless to the corner,
We walked. Before us lay our way – not long.
You gripped my hand; whispered: 'For me, be strong.
A little further…just; no need to hurry.'
'I should be slower with a bag to carry,'
I joked. We came to the bank of the River.
I said: 'You are cold, my love, and shiver.'
As I wrapped my coat around you, darling girl,
A poem fell into the water's run.
    Came one great waft of wind-and-water whirl –
    You stooped…and, looking up, found…I was gone.

14th November, 2014

Enigma

Alan Turing

No answer in Eden ever damned for spite;
No question there but happy curiosity
Which God could cure. Nor did complexity
Or doubt exist until the apple-bite.
But now the questions stack too thick,
And answers are a popular sound-bite
Of what is 'right'. And God is recondite.
And those outside the 'Norm' are fools, or sick.

The valves of my Bombe glow, the rotors wind,
Decrypting war's Enigma into sense.
'Thank you,' they say; 'but for your heart's pretence
You must, dear chap, conform; be re-aligned.'
    So Difference was dealt out to me in spite:
    The answer was another apple-bite.

15th November, 2014

Alan Turing, at Bletchley, built the Bombe machine that decoded the German Enigma messages. In 1952 he was prosecuted for homosexuality, and given the choice of prison or chemical castration. He died two years later probably as a result of suicide. An apple, with a bite out of it, was found beside his body.

'Close' Neighbours

for Dorothy Bartholomew

Dear Dorothy, remember the B.L.Ss
In your Cathedral Close, just down Hook's Walk?
All grubby faces, scruff, and hand-down dresses;
Whole brood of them. Just hear their mother talk…
Well, scream…'Bleeding Little Sods'. She called them
That. But you enjoyed their nonconformity:
Their noisy paper rounds and clapped-out pram;
Were fond of them; invited them to tea.
I have such neighbours now to entertain;
My urchin squad beyond our party-wall
With shindigs late at night. Their name is Payne.
Well, that's a joke. They greet me in the hall
    And grin. They're not uncivil, just outré;
    In time, it may be I shall move away…

9th December, 2014

Moonshine. Low Roofs

Two a.m. Soft moonlight launders sight and soul:
The lawn, the lilac; lace of jasmine leaf
Against the window sill. Patterns unscroll
Over my feet, carpet; over the motif
Of the wardrobe and bed's yew-quartered grain.

The waning moon, with Jupiter to hand,
Spreads space-reflected grace; and spins again
At my old home…the spells of fairyland.

Make-believe blurs; a fading figure stirs.
Now, words of near twelve years might at one stroke
Be unwritten…*(neither my light nor hers*
As yet has reached the stars)…if she awoke.
    On her father's ship sounds… 'Four Bells'…in pairs!
    The sand runs on. The magic…disappears.

11th December, 2014

Shelf Life

for my mother who never begrudged me a good book

Dusting, polishing old books I realise
A truth. Though some have been unwisely lent
And others lost, ranged round me are my spies
On life, with whom delicious hours have spent.
Tried friends: some gifts; armed trophies gilt-embossed;
Others for story, wisdom, wit devoured;
Oft nodded over, fingered, margins glossed.
I know just where to find them, candle-houred
Companions.
                 Not all to read: no need
For either men or books to justify
Their place, but with a neighbourly good grace, plead
For those who sit upon a shelf nearby.
  So, when I dust my books, you will know why.
  Keep them intact. I am my library.

18th January, 2015

Lights Out

The lamps are going out all round my park…
Where I live. Soft gleams that never assume
Ascendency – conformable to dark.
Wick, wax, oil, gas…at eventide commune
With darkness, bestowing gentle ray,
Unlike the modern glare that would strike night
To day, for fear that Fear will come to stay.
The Linkman on his beat snuffs out each light.
Each office, porter's lodge, hall, residence
Follows suit. Shadows gloom; footsteps echo.
'Goodnight sweet ladies; goodnight sweet prince.'
'Time, gentlemen, please. Take care how you go.'
  It seems good sense to practise finding home
  In indistinctness that is bound to come.

11th January, 2015

'I am overtired
Of the great harvest I myself desired'
Robert Frost

A warm, out-of-season day: The lawn spooned
With syrupy dollops of light; bees skate-board
Gaily down noon's sunbeams; their hum new tuned.

From one hive portal, though, none stirs abroad.

Heart sinks. This…my last year's great provider.
I break wax seals to a mausoleum
Furnished with gold, unthieved by the spider.
None here…who courted autumn's ivy bloom.
Not long, but this was forge and busy home,
The throbbing heart, and roar, and teeming womb
Of many thousand shining wings. Now…gloom
And grey-chill silence of the catacomb.
     Their gusto thrilled me all the summer through.
     Have I the energy to start anew?

9th February, 2015

Santa Maria dei Miracoli, Venice

Approaching the altar, the visitor passes directly
between Mary and Gabriel of the Annunciation.

It was, I daresay, like any day
But in that goat-bleating, birdsong dawn
An Angel waited; had dropped by to say
'Thou shalt conceive, and…God's son will be born.'
That 'shalt' and 'will' suggest a done deal,
Pressure! But your sweet maidenly assent
Made all right, and heaven's nearness come real
For us, which is, perhaps, what God once meant.

So climbing steep steps, here, may be a proof
That **you** are picked, whatever your intent:
To view the image, or the coffered roof,
Or kneel before the aumbry's Sacrament?
     For **you** have intervened, all unaware,
     'Tween Angel words and Mary's prayer.

Maundy Thursday, 2015

The Hundredth Yew Tree, Painswick Churchyard

My hundredth sonnet

Try counting them – those Painswick yew-trees clipped
To toad-stool hats, and lollies sucked on sticks.
Ninety…something? The hundred's always pipped
When checked again. The Devil at his tricks,
So local folklore tells. The hundredth yew
He won't allow; will grub it up in glee
Lest rector, sexton, warden should fulfil
Their long-held scheme and claim a victory.
With Nick there's only one way to compete:
The Fun, not Finish, is the truer test.
Best cherished plans will never be complete;
Just pie in sky; goodbye 'Perfectum est'.
    One courts trouble to say a job is done!
    This, then, is ninety-nine; my next is One-o-one.

October, 2014

Cake Baking, after a Medical Check-up

Eggs cracked; four yolks plop dolloped in my mixing
Bowl; each heavier seeming than its weight -
Just like my news. Cabochon-amber eyes fixing
My intent, watching the heart equivocate,
They wallow in the dust-flour of past days
Amongst the yellow chunks of butter-fat.
All weighed. Tasting will test how right it weighs!
There's measured sweetness too. I'm glad of that.
Cooking like Life…so much to be combined!
The rich and raw of each ingredient.
'These cooks,' says Chaucer, 'how they stamp and grind
To turnen substance into accident.'
    Just so. And miracles will rise from this.
    My own Victoria sponge I would not miss.

7th April, 2015

Being and not Being

April Blossom

Here, amid blossom of apple and crab,
I have being, no-being; body, yet none.
Oh, **sense** of scent; **seeing**...yes. Fingered dab
Of pink on the petal; caress of the sun.
No **substance**, though. No **stridency** of Time:
Fifty years done...hundred hence! Tis all one.
Of **weight** or of **will**...nothing is mine...
But a **Presence**, still, when the blossom is gone.
Here, in your arms I have being; though lost
In folds of our holding; insistence of kiss.
Less of body – just so, when Lethe is crossed,
But a **Presence**, still, when blossom we miss.
    Here, Lightness and Love our spirits attain;
    If now, why not in years hence – so, again?

St George's Day, 2015

Baraka

'"Baraka"' my pupil, from fifty years, wrote,
'"Blessed though idle and unprofitable"
Was your theme. Remember? Good word for Scrabble.'
How strange, we abide in expressions remote!
'More than a pleasure,' my father would say
At being thanked, his eyes bright with laughter;
So stands beside me, here, long years after
When I repeat: '...As my father would say'.
This clutched small change of the mind's forgetting
We find in **our** talk. Sudden glints of light;
Memories fizzing from headland to height
Dip-flash in a Portland evening setting.
    A sobering thought that words leave a marker
    Of us; a handshake...down the ages! 'Baraka.'

27th April, 2015

Bach's Little Miracle

for Jon Lee and Adrian Davis

Glissando, then, my music of despair:
While surged the great lung'd breath, tongued heart of God
Around; strong pulsing thrust through moted air:
Intent – to some confirming major chord.
No brittle hope, head-scratchings, feeble start,
But conversation, comforting; where no
One interrupts, nor arm from arm may part.
If Bach is certain, why not I be so?
If God be heard, why then should I not hear?
No need the fugue's complexity to plumb,
'But trust,' Bach says. An answer can appear.
Perhaps. 'Vor deinen Thron...' O God, I come.'
    The pillars rock in quakes of autumn sun;
    Toccatas rive despair, quick, to the bone.

19th September, 2015

Spacecraft

A child is blowing bubbles from a ring,
Intent, he breathes a wambling bagginess;
Unshape; in likeness to...not anything;
A caul which captures rainbows in its stress.
Slowly...with little pursed-lipped puffs, it grows.
Steady! Too rough, he knows, and it will burst
In...shower of suds, and wetness on his nose.
Just right; and...wow! – he has a marvel nursed,
A goblin globe that, with convulsion, frees
Itself, spectacular; and bowls in air.
His face that fragile spacecraft ferries.
I was that child; now am his roundy care.
    I wake this night to dark night everywhere,
    And watch my floating, free, and finished, sphere.

August, 2015

~~~

This is not a poem; but a wordless conversation, overheard, set down; a record of hours. It is a recitative for a defining departure. It has lain in a box for nine years, and only now, as my mother's hundredth birthday approaches, can I bear to take it out and re-live those few days that have coloured my life ever since.

A Blackbird Sings

A blackbird sings
On the chimney top:
Beyond this closed, high-up
Room, a threshold to skies –
Hushed, under eaves –
Where my mother dies.
   The sun on her coverlet weaves
Beckoning patterns of wings.

Beneath…slender-still she lies,
Travelling tenderly bidden
Through ways till now hidden.
   My soul yearns to the faint rise…
To the lean of her love…to weigh,
How best I may,
This breath-taking day;
And the strangeness it brings.

O golden-voiced song,
Strung hosannas of prayer;
Oriflamme banner
Flung into air;
Assured aria
From the music of an undimmed world
Not now so far afield,
Where no note can be wrong.

My heart, though, is wrung,
Unmanned…unstrung;
Gaffed with grief at the stillness
On the bed; at the tress
Of swept hair
Which lies
Silvered-gold on the pillow…there.

Calm…lovely of face,
Girl, young again;
My history…whole, you inhabit.
 Dear pilgrim of grace
Nighing the place, eager in spirit,
Serene is your brow.
As you ferry the pain,
With your name round the prow.

Once more! Oh, how he sings!
No head-scratchings;
No false starts. Each phrase just so,
Con brio;
Exact, ecstatic – to show,
From his vantage view,
Something he knows to be true;
And to ask if I know. Do I know?

 (This singing and your living;
 This silence and your dying;
 Like the conduct of a good intent;
 Like a life of meaning meant –
 Derive from choice –
 'Elegans', 'elegant' –
 Apt, sweetly convincing, as right choice
 Ever is;
 Leaning on the emphasis,
 With a golden voice.)

I strain at each pause
That he may yet sing again;
And so, I pray, dear mother, may you.
 Silence weighs the whispers:
'That hope is vain.'

My fear is (though **you** do not fear)
That this silence of ours will never be broken.
Not after the hush before applause,
Not after my curtain is rung down
And I turn to you for approbation.
 No. Last words are already spoken,
The 'Never' starts here.
And lasting is 'last', and firm-fast.

Dimly distant, in the street,
Life measures to a different beat.
Cries of children hazed in heat
Crowding in some ancient game.
    If anything could induce your staying
It would be the sound of children playing –
Calling, calling you by name.

From the streets, the hills, the skies,
From your belovéd father's seas,
From life-resolving destinies –
The welcomers wing fast.
    Here the wise and darling dead
Gather to your still bedhead –
A pierhead clasp of greetings; and my last
Unspoken, finger-tip goodbyes.

Singing spirit
I am loath to think you know
No more for sure –
Simply…than that love and grief endure.
    If that the total we inherit
Then I could inform you so,
In notes less pure.

Though dressed in black
You have not come to mourn.
Even thus in Galilee you sang
Before my mother's
Faith was born.
    And never she, but would have smiled
To hear that something **other**
That your soul perceives,
Which not redeems my lack
Of faith, but leaves
An earnest – that hope may bloom
In this still room
High under eaves.

4th May, 2003
My mother died on 7th May, 2003
Finished in the week of my Mother's 100th Birthday, 2012

Gannets

It is exact: the year.
I journey westwards;
Cannot but…believe you here
By the bow rail-guard
As the ship dips into the smooth heave
Where your father sailed
Once. Light off water. Gannets.
The Land of Saints.
And a faint green sleeve
Of shore towards.

Now further west than you.
Yet you somewhere further still…
Beyond; and ever will
Outfly, however true,
My course – lacking urgent gannet flight
And spearing steep intent, against
This morning's light,
Toward the Land of Saints.

Towards Rosslare
7th May, 2004

61

The River Thames and Anniversaries

14th December, 2009

This is **our** river. We have made it **ours** –
From source to tidal reach almost complete.
This is our weather: wintry showers,
Grey skies and hard-edged sleet.
We walked ice-crackly banks together
Near fifty years ago
You in your new sheepskin leather
High-muffled for the snow.

At Dorchester – Isis and Thames.
The brown and swirling currents meet
And mingle ancient Celtic names
By iron-age fort and Roman street.
In one sense, there, our journey was begun
From 'Bon voyage' to distant coast.
There, Wittenham Clumps and Sinodun,
And back to fire, hot-buttered toast.

The date the same, but years have passed
And we sit by a fire again.
I in 'Idylls of the King' held fast,
Sir Lancelot and Fair Elaine.
Foolish retreat into Romance,
Shalotting from reality;
Embowered from that slim, dim expanse
That mists us from the sea.

Last steps are where slow waters free
Once more from land, and broaden out to ride
Long rhythms of the estuary,
The coming-to-meet-us drift of tide.
In passaging we've almost walked the course.
Left only are few footling, small gaps…
Between the wide sea-surge and far-off source.
Laughingly we shall leap them – perhaps
      Next year…or next. Perforce.

> *Written at Long Hanborough.*
> *We finished the Thames Walk*
> *just before our*
> *Golden Wedding Anniversary, in 2010*

Barham Down

for W.S-J

Beyond Bridge, the car suddenly slowed,
As if some ancient urge
Had eased it, bumping, off the road
Onto the grassy verge
  Beside a sagging, five-barred
  Gate that opened to a chalk-scarred
 Track, that led up Barham Down.

The driver: gaunt, moustached and grim –
Veteran of gas, shell, and the Somme –
'Buffer'. We were in awe of him,
And his Virgil, Horace, Xenophon.
  Subjunctive mood and compound tense
  I strove to tinker into sense.
 He twitched his ink-stained gown.

But I loved him for taking us to see
The larder of the red-backed shrike –
The butcher bird – a summer rarity;
The jerky-flying green hairstreak
  I watched as with a wristy twist of grip
  He'd lap the female orange tip
 In the black mist of his net.

'Come with me.' And up the track he stalked,
With firm intent. I…left to follow.
He scanned the rough ground chalked
By rabbit holes, each sparse-grazed hollow.
  At last:
  'I saw a grayling here in twenty-eight…
  June,' to himself…'about this date.'
 Encounter never to forget.

Now sixty years have passed by, since
No grayling sunned upon the trefoiled flowers;
All gone that age of innocence,
A thousand longed-for rendezvous.
What remain? Midnight longings to construe
That 'summum bonum' once was ours.

~~~

Little Gidding

Certain places are deft to underwrite our being;
To loop mere moments in the hem of history,
Making us valid in the story because...
We come. Not knowing, quite, why we come;
Turning in and out of winter sun
By a lane that falters, tending nowhere,
But arrives, even so, by going nowhere;
Away from the fake-believe of fact
To an awaked-retrieve of faith. That is
The importance. One has half won simply
By staying true to the coming.
                              A track oblique –
More grass than tarmac. Fields eking with wet
Against a sullen sky. Winter death...though zealous
Featherings of fieldfare from the hedge.
Time of no colour; but of Quaker shades,
The not-snow whiteness of snowdrops
Beside a dark pool. Path slippery for no feet;
Grass bruised with no prints
To a church of no warmth, brass of no
Shine, an iron-bound door excluding no wind;
To an offering bowl with no gift, and the insignia
Of a king who was already not. The only
Determination is in my breath on leaded glass;
My writing in the book for prayers –
I would not wish not to be here; it is enough:
'For Liz, her birthday, with my happy love.'

23rd January, 2014

~~~

David Pearce was born in Whitstable in 1938. That Kentish coastline was, in the early war years, under threat; and for a while, as a small child, he was an evacuee in Cornwall. After school at St Edmund's, Canterbury, and then St Edmund Hall, Oxford, he taught at Stanbridge Earls, Hampshire, and then, for thirty-three years at Berkhamsted School where he was Head of English and a boarding housemaster. He was a joint-founder of the Graham Greene Birthplace Trust, and, through that, rejoices in friends all round the world. The importance of his family life and other interests may be deduced from the poems.

~~~

15664158R00044

Printed in Great Britain
by Amazon